"I Am Always With You,"

Jesus Promises In The Lord's Supper

By Marie Sundet

Illustrated by Sunday School children
of First Lutheran Church,
Cedar Rapids, Iowa

ISBN 1-889407-25-9

"I am always with you." Jesus promises in The Bible. We come to the Lord's Supper after we are baptized.

Jorunn Musil

When we are baptized, we become God's children here on earth. God is our heavenly parent who loves us very much. We are God's family.

Eric Klinsky

Jesus is God's son. He died on the cross to take away our sins. God tells us, "I love you so much that I gave my son, Jesus, to forgive your sins."

Evan Anderson

Sins are things we do that hurt us and hurt other people. God feels bad when we sin, but God forgives our sins. Then we can try to live as God's loving children.

Nicholas Griner

One day after supper, Jesus had an important meeting with his good friends. "Soon I am going to die," he said. "But I will live again. Then I will be with God in heaven. You will not see me, but you need to remember me."

Emily Proffitt

Then he shared some bread and some wine with them. He said "Eat this bread. It is my body. Drink this wine. It is my blood. Do this often to remember me."

Karen Lottes

These words are in the Bible. The Bible is God's word.

Kristen Rooney

The day after this supper, Jesus died. When Jesus died, God gave him new life.

Matthew Jarvey

When we die, God will give us new life. God will say, "Come right in - you're home." Then we will live forever with God in heaven.

Shelby Buckley

The Lord's supper is the time when we eat bread and drink wine. Some of us do this when we are young children. Some of us wait until we are older.

Erin Dick

Whenever we eat the bread and drink the wine, Jesus is with us. We thank God for Jesus.

Nathan Griner

Jesus' love helps us to love other people. He is with us and loves us all of the time. We know this in the Lord's Supper. In the Bible Jesus promises us, "I am always with you."

Kevin Dyrland